Hawai'i

IMAGES OF THE ISLANDS

Photography by
Douglas Peebles

Mutual Publishing

All photos by Douglas Peebles.

ISBN 1-56647-726-3

Library of Congress Catalog Card Number: 2005922204

First Printing, May 2005
1 2 3 4 5 6 7 8 9

Mutual Publishing, LLC
1215 Center Street, Suite 210
Honolulu, Hawai'i 96816
Ph: 808-732-1709 / Fax: 808-734-4094
email: mutual@mutualpublishing.com
www.mutualpublishing.com

Printed in Taiwan

A hike through the Ohiʻa Forest on the island of Kauaʻi uncovers sweeping views and small pleasures, like an up-close glimpse of the famed lehua flower.

The delicate fronds of the taro plant stretch deep into the Kaua'i Refuge Complex.

The carved ridges of the Nāpali Coast rise 4,000 feet straight into the sky.

An endangered species protected by federal and state laws, the green sea turtle
can often be seen swimming in the clear waters of the Pacific.

Windswept palms tower above the changing blues of Kēʻē Beach.

Kīpū Kai Valley, south of Nāwiliwili Bay, is home to a private working cattle ranch.

The northernmost tip of Kīlauea National Wildlife Refuge is one of the few refuges open to the public.

The many layered cliffs of Waimea Canyon hint at the natural history of this oldest main Hawaiian island.

Waterfalls slip through the crevices of Mt. Waiʻaleʻale on Kauaʻi, known as the "wettest spot on earth."

Wailua Falls plunges eighty feet into the cool freshwater pool below.

Rocks dotting the sand of Kalalau Beach seem to glow as the sun sets behind the pali.

Diamond Head, Hawai'i's most well-known landmark on O'ahu, rises up from the sea with Kapi'olani Park at its base and Waikīkī highrises stretching into the distance.

A typically beautiful, sunny day peeks through the cliffs
of the historical Nuʻuanu Pali Lookout.

The Aloha Tower was built in 1926 as a symbol of the Hawaiian Islands, to be remembered by the ships entering and leaving Honolulu Harbor.

Diamond Head and Waikīkī shimmer in the early evening light shortly after sunset.

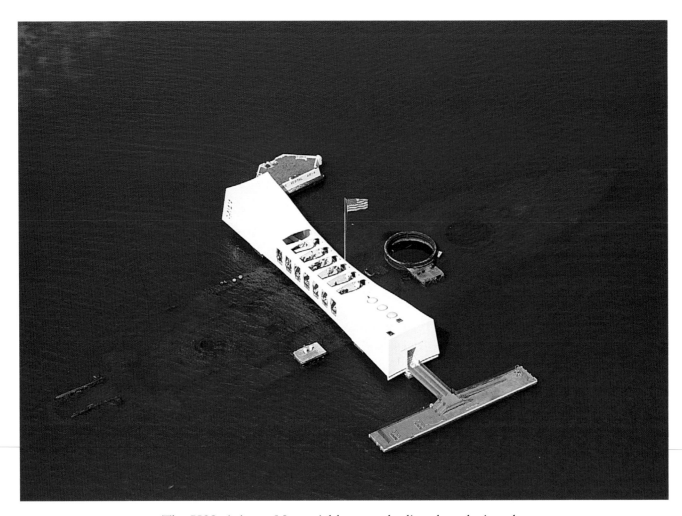

The USS *Arizona* Memorial honors the lives lost during the
attack on Pearl Harbor in World War II.

Punchbowl Crater, also known as Pūowaina, is home to the
National Memorial Cemetery of the Pacific.

Teeming with unusual fishes, the crescent shores of Hanauma Bay is a popular recreational spot for swimming and snorkeling on O'ahu.

Surfers ride the challenge of a powerful wave on the North Shore.

Known for its tranquil surroundings and world-class resort and spa, the beautiful Koʻolina coast of west Oʻahu is one of the best places to relax and enjoy paradise.

A bird's-eye view of Kāneʻohe Bay reveals the Windward side of Oʻahu.

The sun sets in brilliant oranges and yellows at Waikīkī.

A sunny day at Oneloa Beach (Big Beach, Mākena) on the island of Maui entices
locals and tourists to play in the water.

In the quiet of the sea swims a lone honu, or Hawaiian green sea turtle.

A Hawaiian Monk Seal lazily snoozes and suns itself on Wailua beach.

Molokini, off the coast of Maui, is a favorite mooring spot for day diving charters.

A humpback whale plays in the waters of Lahaina.

Among the hottest rides on Maui is the downhill bicycle run from the summit of Haleakalā.

Cinder cones dot the dry interior landscape of Haleakalā.

A sunset glows at Keʻanae Peninsula in Hāna.

Olinda offers the lush countryside of Maui.

Lahaina is a charming waterfront town popular with tourists.

Hula dancers perform a kahiko (ancient hula) at Wai'ānapanapa, a black sand beach on Maui.

Ki'i images, or god figures, can be found at Pu'uhonua o Hōnaunau on the Big Island of Hawai'i.

Puʻuhonua, where the City of Refuge National Historical Park is located, fittingly means "a place of refuge."

A hawksbill turtle—a rare and endangered species—rests on the black sand at Punaluʻu Beach.

Waterfalls cascade down the North Kohala Coast from Waipiʻo to Pololū Valley.

Once rich in native vegetation, the slopes of Hāmākua Coast today are cast mostly with foreign plants and trees that have been introduced to the area.

On a typical day, a cruise ship sits offshore surrounded by small pleasure craft by the Kailua-Kona coastline.

The countryside of Waimea exudes idyllic charm.

Kīlauea Volcano erupts a lava stream, which will eventually flow into the ocean.

Fast-moving rivers of volcanic lava from a Kīlauea eruption glow in the steamy air.

Photographers brave the heat from Kīlauea's eruption to capture rare, close-up images of lava.

Snow-capped Mauna Kea looks as if it is floating amongst the clouds.

The *Hōkūleʻa*, one of Hawaiʻi's most famous voyaging vessels, is at home on the sea.